Knife Making Book for Beginners

A Bladesmithing User Guide to Forging Knives Plus Tips, Tools and Techniques to Get You Started

By

Luke Wade

Copyright © 2021 – Luke Wade

All rights reserved

No part of this publication may be reproduced, distributed, or transmitted in any form or by any means, including photocopying, recording, or other electronic or mechanical methods, without the prior written permission of the publisher, except in the case of brief quotations embodied in reviews and certain other non-commercial uses permitted by copyright law.

Disclaimer

This publication is designed to provide competent and reliable information regarding the subject matter covered. However, the views expressed in this publication are those of the author alone, and should not be taken as expert instruction or professional advice. The reader is responsible for his or her own actions.

The author hereby disclaims any responsibility or liability whatsoever that is incurred from the use or application of the contents of this publication by the purchaser or reader. The purchaser or reader is hereby responsible for his or her own actions.

Table of Contents

Introduction 6

Chapter 1 8

What is Knife Making? 8

    History of Knife Making 8

    How Does Knife Making Work? 10

    Is Knife Making Profitable? - From Hobby to Business ... 13

    Are Custom Knives Worth the Money? 19

    Handmade knives Vs. Factory Knives - Which is Better? 21

Chapter 2 28

Basic Knife Making Terminology 28

Chapter 3 34

Tips and Tricks of Knife Making 34

Chapter 4 38

Getting Started with Knife Making 38

    Knife Forging Vs. Knife Stock Removal 39

Tools and Supplies for Your Workspace 41

    Forge 42

    Anvil 44

    Anvil Stand 48

    Hammer 49

    Tongs 50

    Water Trough 52

    Workbench 54

    Drill 55

    Files 56

    Belt Grinder 58

    Quenchant 59

    Hacksaw 60

    Angle Grinder 60

Knife Making Safety Rules and Equipments 61

Setting Up Your Bladesmithing Workspace 66

Chapter 5 69

Designing Your Knife 69

Anatomy of a Knife 72

    Basic Knife Anatomy 75

    Advanced Knife Anatomy 78

Blade Profiles of a Knife 80

Creating a Knife Template 85

Chapter 6 90

Forging Method of Knife Making 90

    Understanding and Selecting Steel 90

    Cutting Knife Blanks 97

    Grinding the Knife Blanks 97

    Heat Treating the Knife Blanks 98

    Making a Handle for the Knife 103

    Sharpening and Caring for Your Knife 109

Chapter 7 117

Troubleshooting Common Knife Making Problems 117

Chapter 8 126

Knife Making Frequently Asked Questions (Q&A) 126

Conclusion 132

Introduction

Knife making is the process of making knives for different purposes and through several means. The business aspect of knife making will continue to remain for years to come because of its increasing demand and use by all and sundry.

Knifemaking involves the art of using steel to make sharp blades and wooden or plastic material to make handles. The procedures in making knives are simple only if equipped with the right information.

Without the needed materials, you will be unable to make knives either for personal or commercial purposes. Also, during the knife making process, it is necessary to be careful because knife making involves some risky activities like honing and so on.

This book, **Knife Making Book for Beginners,** a step-by-step beginner-friendly guide, aims to equip you with virtually all the knowledge and information you need to kickstart your knife making process and knife making business in the simplest form.

Ready to gear up for an adventurous journey to become a master bladesmith?

Then, see you on the next page!

Chapter 1

What is Knife Making?

Knife making is the act of manufacturing or producing a knife through a sequence of stock removal or welded lamination. Likewise, it is the process of making an edge and sharp tool used for cutting such things as clothes, food items, and so much more.

The main metals used in knife making are usually made from carbon and stainless steel.

History of Knife Making

Without a doubt, the original set of knife makers were early people who lived in the world several years back. It was seen that the early knife makers lived in caves for ages.

Now, why did the knife makers create or combine materials to make knives? The simple answer is that they used it as a means of livelihood, to hunt for wild and home animals in the forest. The earliest human forms sought tools, a strong one at that, to achieve their means of livelihood. What they did to further their livelihood was gather the needed materials to manufacture a knife. Around 5000 – 2000 BC, the early knife makers began refining and enhancing their stone-like knives to get sharper edges. They also went ahead to create the handles as well.

The original iron blades were manufactured out of copper and bronze and they were first seen between 3000 – 700 BC. According to a research study, the first iron blades made were preferred more than those made of stone for some reason.

Fast forward to 1000 BC, metal knives began to gain momentum because they were known to be sharper and long-lasting than the former metals. Human beings have made different kinds of knives in the modern-day knife making process compared to those made in previous years. Different knife making industries are making knives out of carbon steel, alloy steel, tool steel, Damascus steel, and stainless steel in the current world. However, the likes of obsidian, titanium alloys, plastic, cobalt, and ceramics are also used to make knives. It is important to mention that stainless steel is the commonly used material for manufacturing knives because it has a good maintenance property and is easy to use.

How Does Knife Making Work?

Knife making is a technical method of producing knives using metals and applying some techniques to the process. Majorly one can make a knife by forging or stock removal; check out the typical process of making knives as given below.

1. Make out a sketch of a knife on a paper

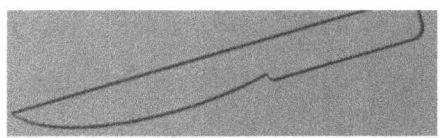

On a sketch paper or graph, draw out the blade, its design, and its intending function, sketch out the blade length, decide how the tangs would look, and sketch out the likely pattern of the knife handle.

2. Purchase your equipment and material

There are tools required to make knives; the tools are in varieties, and their purchase depends on the knife maker. Such tools, for example, are grinder, quenchant, among others. Some are handled manually, and some are automatic. When it comes to materials used in making knives, blades are produced from metals like steel, iron, copper, bronze; the knife function determines the kind of metal to be used. The knife handle also comes in different materials; some are wooden, plastic, or even metal.

3. Forge

Metals are heated in a fire; this is a treatment method used to add more quality to a blade. There are a plethora of forge methods; some are gas-fired, some coal-fired. After firing, the blade is cooled off using water or oil in a water trough. Although some blade smith no longer work with this method, it, however, adds value to the blade and hardens the blade.

4. Trace out the blade

This is a method particular to the stock removal technique. After sketching out a blade drawing on paper, you may trace it out on a slab, which will help cut the metal. After tracing out on a slab, use the slab as a guideline and trace it on the metal.

5. Cut out the traced part of the metal

At this point, you cut out the sketched out part of the metal, which would be used for the knife itself. Advisably, a little space should be included in the metal should in case any mistake occurs during cutting.

In knife making and blacksmithing related practice, a hacksaw is used for cutting metal. Cutting also applies to the knife handles after sketching.

6. Grind the metal

After cutting the traced part of the metal, it is then ground using a grinder. Grinding is a stock removal technique used to shape and smooth metal. There is grinding for shaping the blade sides and that for general smoothing. While grinding, it is advisable to do it with caution to avoid damaging the blade.

7. Make a rivet hole

This is the penultimate stage of making a knife, after doing the necessary blade carvings and adjustments. Drilling a rivet hole on the tang of the blade is the last phase. It is with this rivet hole that the knife handle is attached to a knife. This is done with a drilling machine. The number of holes to be drilled depends on the size of the knife and the kind of handle.

8. Sand the blade

Where a metal was not forged, this is an alternative means for making a blade look shiny and polished. It is done using sandpaper. There are also some finishing touches like designs added to a blade and knife handle.

In subsequent chapters of this book, we will delve deeply into the process of knife making, afterall, that's what this book is all about.

Is Knife Making Profitable? - From Hobby to Business

Without a doubt, most people are anxious to make fast money, but that shouldn't be the case because no good thing comes easy. Since the start of 20 century, knife making has attracted lots of attention from people worldwide. When you hit the internet to look for custom made knives, you should expect to see a few knives selling between 100 – 10,000 dollars and more.

These figures may interest you and make you ask whether knife making can give you the above shocking figures in a short period?

The truth is that knife making is a very profitable business, but it requires you to invest more than enough energy and time. In knife making business, the most essential factors to consider is being aware of the target market and having enough passion.

Some people take knife making as a full-time business; they earn between 30,000 – 200,000 dollars annually. Meanwhile, for others, knife making business is only a means of survival as they may barely manage to make some sales in a month.

Undoubtedly, you have to devout your time and work harder when you seek to grow a profitable knife making business.

Making a Successful Knife Making Business

Just as it applies with other successful businesses, it takes patience and consistency to build. You cannot turn up in the morning and expect to succeed in a short period without doing the necessary work. In fact, if you confirm from anybody in the knife making enterprise, you would be told that the needed work must be done.

Look at a few distinguishing factors that differentiate a successful and skilled knife maker from the rest:

- Understanding the market
- Consistent learning and increasing knowledge concerning knives
- Passion about making knives

- Been experienced a little about knife making

From the above bullet point, let's take the time to break the list into simple terms.

Understanding the knife marketplace is the foremost step to developing a successful knife making business. For example, assuming you like producing fishing knives, you only get a single buyer even after several months of knife making.

On a second thought, assuming you have 15 customers patronizing you for kitchen knives monthly, you must be sure where you stand and what will benefit you.

Even though it may seem that the latter option might be the top-notch plan, several individuals still make this same mistake. Rather than focusing on making more kitchen knives, people will still opt to make fishing knives for reasons best known to them.

To the fishing knife makers, the process of making that particular knife may be easier, hence, their reason for making the fishing knives. The problem may be that they are unlikely to sell unless they opt to manufacture knives that are making sales.

As a person that makes a knife, you must comprehend the law of supply and demand, and it will determine your success in your business. The second critical mistake many knives make is making highly costly knives hoping that people will gather and buy; this should be highly avoided because you cannot build your business based on hope.

A successful knife making business should be built based on understanding the business and making things that will possibly attract the public. Imagine making a particular costly knife and selling it in your local store where most residents there are not financially capable; who do you expect to buy the knives?

Understanding and following the business of knife making will guarantee you sales and profit, respectively.

Consistent learning and increasing your idea in the art of knife making will aid you as you seek to venture into the business. You cannot remain stagnant in your knowledge concerning knives, especially if you seek to make any headway in your business.

To be an established knife maker, one should be willing to keep on learning and increase your awareness about knives. Other things one should learn about knife making could be how to make attractive knives, create a perfect handle, know the type of selling knives, and so much more.

Before venturing into any business, you should ensure you have some **level of passion**; else your business will not move forward. Without having the right passion, you may only but make fewer knives than you planned before entering knife making as a venture. It is necessary to love what you do, if not, you will gradually lose interest in the knife enterprise in a short time without commanding the market.

If you start any business with the sole aim of making money without working hard, you will not get far. Do not forget the reason you began making knives. Definitely, you will have some days where you won't feel like making knives or even selling, which is fine because everyone has such days as well. However, your mindset must be set right to keep on going, notwithstanding your feeling towards making knives.

The last point you must seek to have is to gain a little or decent **experience in making knives** before venturing into your knife making business. It requires you to devote some time and consistent practice to be a guru or an expert in the business.

Once you know the ways to produce a perfect knife before starting the business, you are already on the path to becoming successful at the skill. There are some things to always consider regarding knife making, including the design, right heat treatment, choice of material, balance, and so much more.

For some people, when they started making knives, they made inquiries and sought information from the most experienced ones. This is also what you should do to ensure your knife making business flourishes.

You don't necessarily have to experience failure or make mistakes; you can seek mentoring from people who have previously failed in the craft and became successful after correcting their mistakes.

Once you can follow the above steps, you are just a few steps away from hitting your first deal and making your first sale. All successful knife making business started as a passion and went ahead to be a business.

As we round up this section, it is imperative to be aware that manufacturing a knife for a friend or family member is also different from making a knife and selling it to a customer.

Are Custom Knives Worth the Money?

It is important to know that knives are not to be referred to as commodities. Assuming a regular knife worth 50$ and a custom knife worth 500$, it does not make the custom knife way better than the regular knife.

The custom knife might only surpass the regular knife by 15%, although it varies on the steel type used in making knives. Once the custom knife production is completed, a bladesmith is not concerned about the price of the material used because an individual who can pay for it won't be bothered about spending an additional 100$.

So, why are custom knives so expensive than regular knives?

Customers must bear in mind that purchasing a custom knife means buying the craft of a skillful and talented knife maker. A custom knife is perfect for you and every need you may want to use it for.

Another distinguishing factor that differentiates custom and industrial knives is the concentration of detail provided. You cannot find any machine that will cover up for a skillful and experienced bladesmith in terms of fine-tuning.

If you look at the industrial and custom knives, they may appear the same, but some attributes distinguish one from the other. For example, the major difference is that a custom knife is manufactured in detail. Meanwhile, for people that need a regular knife for the everyday need of cutting food items, a custom knife is not needed, and it is not necessary.

On the contrary, assuming you are a lover of a knife, knife collector, or professional knife operator, then paying heavily for a custom knife will worth it.

Do you want to make or even buy a custom knife? You should understand that it comes at diverse prices. Some of which includes:

- The least you can purchase a custom knife is between 50 – 500$
- Other custom knives are estimated between 500 – 2000$
- While the top-notch custom knives are valued at more than 2000$

Handmade knives Vs. Factory Knives - Which is Better?

Handmade Knife

Handmade knives are much better than factory knives. Although you may argue because factory knives are produced in factories, there are reasons behind the choice to highly rate handmade knives.

Below are a few factors that make handmade knives highly rated:

- Price
- Sharpness
- Material
- Durability
- Design

Price

Undoubtedly, price is a significant factor most people consider when buying a knife. Assuming you are not financially buoyant, you should opt for an industrially made knife because they are less costly.

Nevertheless, assuming you are a professional or knife lover, you necessarily need to get a handmade knife. Although they may be expensive, they are certainly worth going for.

In other words, you should likewise consider the price of your knife if you intend to venture into the knife making and selling business.

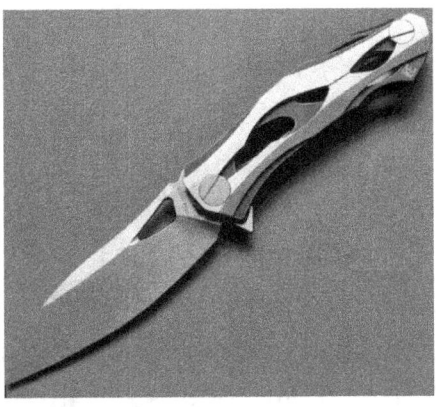

Factory-made Knife

Sharpness

Sharpness is among the clear and palpable reasons why people purchase knives; one you must also consider when making your own knife be it for personal use or for business purposes. Assuming a knife cannot cut certain things, would you purchase it? Well, most people wouldn't.

Most factory-made knives have sharp edges, but the only problem they have is their durability status. Because they are not forged, that makes them very flexible, and their edges stay for a shorter time than a handmade knife.

In comparison with a handmade knife, it is so flexible, and it makes it very sharp. Handmade knives are forged, hence the reason they are strong and hard.

Material

A good material will make a great knife. The durability and efficiency of a god knife are dependent on good material. Virtually every handmade knife is manufactured from Damascus steel, high-carbon steel, or stainless steel.

All these steels are made of high-quality materials and no wonder why they are used for knife making. In a different vein, factory-made knives do not use the above-listed steels. Some factory-made knives are without steel.

Durability

This is also a crucial factor to determine whenever you seek to make or get a knife. In normal circumstances, a handmade knife is more durable because it is forged. Furthermore, handmade knives can serve up to an extended period without running out of sharpness.

Lastly, handmade knives are very flexible, hence, their easiness in sharpening things.

Design

Knife designs may not be so important, but they are still a deciding factor to consider when making or buying knives. As regards factory-made knives, they usually consider quantity over quality. This shouldn't happen because quality also plays a part in why people buy different things, including knives.

Workers in a knife factory are always given a daily target to manufacture knives that they must reach before closing for the day. So, to reach their daily target, they often develop fewer quality knives to meet up the demands of knives given for that day.

However, handmade knives focus on the need for detail and quality. Thus, the reasons a majority of handmade knives usually have a nice design than factory-made knives.

Advantages of handmade knives

- **Longer lasting:** Every handmade knife features a better durability feature because of its need for detail.
- **Nice design:** As stated above, handmade knives focus on quality rather than quantity. A top-notch knife will always have a nice and attractive design.
- **Sharper:** Unlike factory-made knives where the edges are only sharp for a short period, handmade knives have much sharper edges that last for long periods.
- **Quality material:** Handmade knife makers use quality and most expensive materials to manufacture knives.

- **Manufactured with attention to detail:** Instead of manufacturing any knife type, the handmade knife makers seek to concentrate detail to manufacture top-notch knives that will make people pay heavily to get.

Downsides of handmade knives

- **Costly:** The only disadvantage of getting a handmade knife is that it is expensive. However, the cost of purchasing or making a handmade knife should be your worry because it is worth it.

Advantages of factory-made knives

- **Cheap:** If you are within a budget or don't want to exhaust your cash buying knives, you can stick with a factory-made knife. A factory-made knife is produced for those who prefer to use a regular knife and not a sophisticated knife. As a knife maker, this should also be part of your consideration.
- **Readily available:** Since the factory-made knife is cheap to purchase, most markets will sell it to the public. Unlike handmade knives where it is hard

to get the materials to make, factory-made knife makers use cheap materials to make more knives to sell.

Disadvantages of factory-made knives

- **Basic design:** Industrial produced knives are simply made with just the normal design you will find in a regular knife. Their makers do not seek to entice the customers but only to sell more knives with the hope of making more profit.
- **Poor durability:** Most factories made knives do not last as long as the handmade knives. This is mostly because factory-made knives are made with low-quality materials. So with a factory-made knife, you should not expect the edges to be as sharp as they used to when you first bought it.
- **Lack of attention to detail:** Factory-made knives also fail to concentrate on the necessary details while producing knives to be sold. This lack of attention to detail seen in a factory-made knife is one reason why it is not good enough compared to handmade knives.

Chapter 2

Basic Knife Making Terminology

As a bladesmith seeking to select the right materials for your knife production venture or hobby, it is best you get familiar with the different terminologies surrounding them.

These basic knife making terminologies will make you know when someone mentions something related to the art of making a knife. It will also bring you into the limelight of different knife making materials and tools.

Look below to understand the different and basic knife making terminologies:

1. **Blade:** The blade is the common fragment of a knife that everyone should know about. Blades are not merely seen in knives but in everything that can cut things. To easily recognize the blade in a knife, gaze around the edges for a sharp metal part. The essence of a blade in a knife is especially for cutting or slicing things, including cotton, paper, etc.

2. **Back:** The back is a term in a knife used to refer to the unsharpened part of the metal blade. For some people, it is often seen as the spine of the knife. The back of a knife does not serve any function, but it is there to enhance a bit of gloss to the knife.
3. **Belly:** Yes, you may wonder what portion of the knife is referred to as the belly. The belly is seen as the curved edge of the blade in a knife. All worthy knife has a curved edge.
4. **Bolster:** The bolster is a part of metal included in the handle for additional decoration or strength. Usually, if you check the upper part of the guard in a knife, you will find a bit of metal added to the handle. This handle provides extra support when handling a knife and augments the decoration of the knife.
5. **Carbon:** Carbon is a common material used for making knife blades. Carbon is stress-free to sharpen into an edge and not steel. But then again, it is more inclined to deteriorate if appropriate care is not taken.

6. **Bail:** The bail is a metal half-loop used to bind or secure the knife to move it with ease. Instead of finding it problematic to lift the knife, the bail helps to clip the knife for easy carry.
7. **Epoxy:** Epoxy is seen as the binding mediator used to join the different portions of a knife. Epoxy is usually made from amino resin or polyamide. This polyamide and amino resin are united with a hardening agent.
8. **Damascus steel:** The Damascus steel is composed of two kinds of steel being folded continuously while the forging process is on-going. This makes it last for an extended period than two original sheets of steel.
9. **Guard:** The guard is the portion of the knife that divides the handle from the blade. In return, this protects the hand from coming in contact with the knife itself. The guard is also referred to as the hilt.

10. **Edge:** The edge is also a common part of the knife. It is referred to as the sharpened part of the blade in the knife.
11. **Micarta:** Micarta is a material used in making handles in a knife. It is generally made from laminates, wood, paper, or linen and mixed with phenolic resin.
12. **Inlays:** They are materials decorated into a knife's handle.
13. **Pins:** As we all know, pins are little pieces of copper or brass used to join tangs, scales, and other knife portions together.
14. **Liner:** This is the inner segment of the handle. Liners are made from soft metals. It serves the function of protecting a blade from damaging especially when it is covered.
15. **Pommel:** Pommel is referred to as an extension or knob seen at the edge of a knife's handle. It also offers additional support to the knife's handle.
16. **Ricasso:** This is the unsharpened area of the knife's blade seen underneath the guard.

17. **Scales:** Scales are small pieces of horn, synthetic material, or wood that are engrossed or pinned to the tang.
18. **Retention:** The retention shows or reveals how excellently or poorly the blade holds an edge.
19. **Rockwell Hardness Test:** This is acknowledged as the typical test for knowing the hardness of a blade's steel. To determine this, a diamond point is placed into the tip of a blade, and the penetration level is determined.
20. **Scrimshaw:** This is a form of art whereby knife handles are created from bone or any other soft materials. It has small holes in them which are covered with ink to form a patterned design.
21. **Spine:** Spine is another name that refers to the back of the knife.
22. **Shield:** It is a metal inlay usually seen on the knife's handle.
23. **Tang:** It is a portion of the knife that spreads to the handle.
24. **Stainless steel:** It is not like the standard steel with a lesser amount of chromium and high

carbon. In stainless steel, the chromium is high while the carbon level is low.

25. **Temper:** It is a process of heating the steel again and again to raise its hardness.
26. **Pakkawood:** It refers to several layers of birch veneers or maple that have color and resin, mixed with pressure and increased heat.

Chapter 3

Tips and Tricks of Knife Making

In most cases, good bladesmiths are known by how they conduct or carry out their knife craft professionally. This professional conduct is a result of some tricks and tips which they work with.

When we say tips and tricks of making a knife, we mean hints, advice new knife makers must follow in other to last long in the enterprise of making knives. The majority of the hints became known due to the experiences of experts; they now serve as advice to starters. Some helpful tips and tricks can be seen below:

1. Sketch before starting the knife making process

This applies mainly to those that use the knife stock removal process. It reduces extra time on knife making and also prevents unnecessary wastage of metal materials. On a sketch paper, size, the shape is drawn; this aids in giving foresight before scrapping or grinding out fractions of the metal.

2. Always get materials ready before starting

Knife makers must get their equipment and materials work ready before starting a knife making process. It is bizarre for a bladesmith not to have prepared his workshop before working or even testing some of his tools. It causes low productivity, confusion, and even accident in a workshop.

3. **Ensure to get original materials**

If you are considering venturing into the knife making craft, how well people will patronize you relies on the standard and the originality of material used in making your knife. Even though there may be no clear standard of a fake or original material, the most definite thing is that people would buy what they know would last long for them.

4. **Try to be artistic**

Customers often look out for attractive knives as their choice; therefore, it is necessary to be artistic as a knife maker. For those who use forging for making knives, adequate heating makes the blade strong and shiny.

A well-polished knife also captures people's interest; all blade smiths should be artistically creative so that their knife will not look like a random metallic blade. Other things people check out for in terms of the beauty of a knife is the handle, the color, style e.t.c

For more tips and hints, kindly refer to the section in chapter 1; *Is Knife Making Profitable? - From Hobby to Business,* I believe we discussed extensively some tips that will come handy for anyone who wants to venture into making knives.

A Short message from the Author:

Hey, I hope you are enjoying the book? I would love to hear your thoughts!

Many readers do not know how hard reviews are to come by and how much they help an author.

I would be incredibly grateful if you could take just 60 seconds to write a short review on Amazon, even if it is a few sentences!

>> Click here to leave a quick review

Thanks for the time taken to share your thoughts!

Chapter 4

Getting Started with Knife Making

Knife making is all about the production of a knife through some blacksmithing procedures. Metals are forged to the desired shape, and cast wielded. It may also undergo a process of stock removal. Knife blades could be made from iron, stainless steel, copper, brass, and carbon steel, among others.

Materials gotten are differently applied and treated for making knives; this is due to their nature. Metals undergo toughness, edge retention, hardness, sharpness, and corrosive resistance. When a metal intended for a blade is shaped, this process is called forging. The material passes through a certain degree of heat temperature; the material could be hammered into desired shapes at this level. The metal could be forged through bending or folding in an artistic design. Other procedures involved in the making of knives, as earlier mentioned, includes knife stock removal.

As knife makers, we might often be wrong in our calculations in the cutting of metals; there are probably a few unwanted patterns. In other to avoid the stress involved in the forging and re-forging of knives, blacksmiths introduced the stock removal technique. Stock removal is synonymous with carving; in this process, parts in a blade not needed are scrapped off until a knife is formed.

Let's delve more into the techniques of knife forging and knife stock removal.

Knife Forging Vs. Knife Stock Removal

In the blacksmithing world, just like every other profession, there are different opinions regarding choice and contentious facts. Some may buy into a particular idea, philosophy, or even standards, while others may object and suggest a contradictory opinion. Knife making is not also left out in this issue of taking sides; this is because of the difference in blacksmiths' mode of working. We shall analyze why the knife forging technique and knife stock removal is often compared.

Knife forging has been in existent even to this day, which is among several reasons people adopt the forging method. Asides from this, it is more traditional. Reversely, stock removal is a product of technological advancement; hence it's simply a new technique. Talking about time consumption, for people without patience or who would not spend the whole day making knives, stock removal is a choice for them. Knife stock removal is less time-consuming, unlike forging, which requires numerous processes before a knife is made.

In the area of material management, knife makers begin to hammer off or cut off parts not needed after heating and firing. However, those who use the stock removal process only need to purchase materials that are nearly the same size as how their knife would be and scrap off the unneeded part. Stock removal is less stressful because technological innovations aid its making process, for example, using grinding machines and the likes.

Another factor often considered by people is the durability standard that may result from the manufacturing knives using any of the methods. Knife forging scientifically yields long-lasting blades because of the process it undergoes; metals are cast and fired. In this process, some strong chemical build-ups are formed that build it up. For stock removal, metals do not undergo any of such treatment; materials are just used directly when they get purchased.

Forging requires great skill and craftsmanship, which many individuals prefer not to venture into. It needs experience and comprehensive tutoring from experienced blacksmiths. Manufacturing knives via the forging method is so delicate because a little mistake can nullify the entire procedure; hence you require adequate learning and mastery.

However, stock removal does not require a lot of learning, experience, and mastery compared to forging; mechanized equipment has helped to a great degree in that regard. What is required is to study the manual on handling the machinery, requiring patience and artistry. Many who would take knife making would opt for knife stock removal due to its consistent supply to the market.

Tools and Supplies for Your Workspace

Forge

A forge is a hearth used for burning or heating materials at a very high temperature till it becomes easier to shape into the desired form. In other words, a forge can be defined as a stone-lined furnace where metals are well heated before taken to the anvil for hammering. In a case whereby the forge is indoors or in an enclosed place, a small vent will have to be set up in the ceiling to guide the smoke and ash away from the room. The vent will help to ensure the room is always conducive and comfortable, especially when the forge is in use. Every forge has a blower that helps to blow air from underneath onto hot coals. A forge could also be referred to as a place where the hearth or furnace is located.

Types of Forge for Knife Making

Charcoal forge: This forge-type uses coal to fire up metallic materials. This is a mapped out place where the fire is being fuelled in large amount with coals, having a furnace.

Gas forge: Natural gas is used as fuel to fire up metals. Unlike the charcoal forge, metals here are heated with a cylindrical container and a gas burner. The cylindrical container is ceramic in texture; there are different sizes of a gas forge.

Finery Forge: This forge-type is similar to an iron refinery where iron ore is transformed into wrought iron with reduced carbon, using a plant or mill powered by water.

Best Forge for Knife Making

You cannot find a precise answer to this question because opinions are relative to this topic. Some people may prefer a particular forge because of its health implications, time, or method. As such, there are several factors in deciding the best forge-type, which might not necessarily be in coherence with another knife maker's factor. However, in the overall sense, many would go for gas forge because it has little health implications. Its propane level burns faster and could also be improvised in one's home in cases of eventuality.

A gas forge is also prone to fire outbreaks as a result of carelessness, which may be devastating if it is not adequately contained. But with fire extinguishers and gas leak check technology, the risk of fire outbreaks using gas forge can be reduced.

Anvil

This tool is an essential tool for making knives, and for one to reach the stage in which he or she can operate the anvil, an advanced understanding of making knives is needed, experience, and better tutorship. Unlike some other knife making tools, the anvil is one of the few used for forging purposes.

It is solid metal with a block-like shape, and a plain surface, and curved sides that allow a metallic object to be designed, reconstructed, or hammered. The idea and brain behind the anvil is that it aided ancient blacksmiths in forging objects into shapes of their choice when there were no modern blacksmithing tools in such primitive times.

Notwithstanding, today's anvil is a bit different, unlike before, due to technological advancement. Some are now made up of cast steel that has been treated with electric induction, flame, or fire.

Anvil features a hard flat surface; its hardness helps to withstand gravity and reduces its potential for deformity.

- It is uniquely designed with round edges, really curvy.
- It has a horn-like shoot-out, which is not so hardened in nature, although it is made of metal.
- It has a small step, somewhere around the face and the horn projection.
- There is a provision where some particular objects are cut and forged. It is referred to as the hard hole, square in shape.

You would also find blocks are called upsetting. Although you can find this in modern anvils, it is otherwise known as an upsetting block.

Other features include the pritchel hole, a rare feature found only on modern anvils.

In this paragraph, you would be taught how to operate the anvil properly, using its different features.

The flat surface is the basic and probably the important part of the anvil. Due to its hardened nature, an object can be hammered on it without fear. It has a flat surface because, in the process of hammering, any carving on the surface would automatically be transferred to the steel being hammered on.

More importantly, hammers should not have a direct connection with the surface to increase their work span. The round curvy edges are usually sharp and cause the metal worked upon to break if it comes into contact with it. Blacksmiths professionally use it when you have to create a break or a cut on the object under work.

The horn is cone-like in shape, projected outward. Round and curvy shapes are forged using the horn projection, it helps to bend the object and so forth. It is not so metallic or hardened. As mentioned above, the small step can be located in the middle of the horn and the surface. It is a sharp cutter, ensuring that the surface is not exposed to damage because of cutting. Hence the step prevents the chisel and the surface from quick damage that may result due to cut. Generally, the step is soft.

Some objects are difficult to cut and forged, which may pose delay and unnecessary stress on the smither. Those objects are worked on using the hard hole for cutting or bending. Where there is a need for an object to be reduced in length and thickness, the upsetting block is used.

An object may often be long and tiny, becoming useless; the upsetting block reduces the length and relatively makes it thicker. Pritchel hole aids for the opening of holes and punching on the most metallic object.

Looking at the function of the anvil, metal could be flattened into a knife, bent, curved, and even be punctured.

Anvil Stand

An anvil stand is a raised platform used by blacksmiths to support the anvil and make them comfortable when hammering metal. It is more healthy, reduces back stress, movable, and customizable. The stand is generally portable; its portability is because of modernization, unlike in the old days.

Anvil stand includes additional space for extra tools that helps in the easy location of blacksmithing tools. Sometimes stands come in wooden shape, and sometimes it comes in a metal shape. It has no special essence other than it helps in using the anvil easily. A stand helps to hold the anvil tight when a heavy metal is hammered.

Hammer

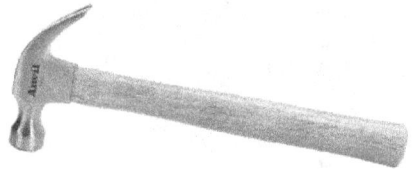

A hammer is an essential tool, with a long handle and a sizeable head. It is carried and used in a way that leaves a mark on the object. Regarding forging and making knives, it is heavily hit on the metal object to either flatten it or shape it.

Although hammers in recent times are not as they were in the ancient days, they are now stronger, heavier, and hardened; thus, you should use them with caution, in order not to touch the anvil because it could lead to damage.

To comprehensively understand the concept of the hammer tool, you can find different kinds of hammers, and some may not necessarily be suitable for blacksmithing due to their soft nature.

However, you can see a few hammers distinctively designed for a purpose like blacksmithing. For instance, the ball-peen hammer, brick hammer (originally for construction purpose), and sledgehammer, to mention but a few.

Generally, the hammer's handle is either made of wood, rubber, and metal, depending on the kind of hammer. Some electrical hammer includes powered steam hammers and trip hammers. The function of the hammer in knife making can not be overemphasized.

To reduce hazards and risks that may arise during hammering, you should tighten the hammer hard in case it is loosed. Knife making and general blacksmithing require full gravity when using the hammer; hence a loosed head in most cases may result in life-threatening injuries. Adhesives could be used to tighten a loose hammer.

Tongs

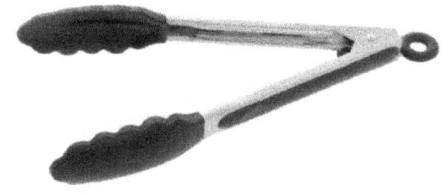

It is a V-shaped tool used by blacksmiths to bring out a heated metal from a fire furnace. It has two arms that could be moved at just one end, holding onto things firmly. Tongs prevent individuals from directly holding something that may cause injury to them. Specially created for picking up a delicate object, the tong is used widely by different professionals.

There are tongs for picking up metals from fire, coals, serving of foods, and so on. The main focus is on its importance or link with knife making. Sometimes, the heating of metals may occur before hammering; in whichever way a smither desires to go about it, he uses a tong to bring the metal from the fire. It is often used to change the metal in different directions inside the fire so that its different parts could be heated adequately.

In a specific manner, tongs with a pivotal and gripping end are often used for blacksmithing, unlike some other kinds of tongs that can handle only cooking functions.

Water Trough

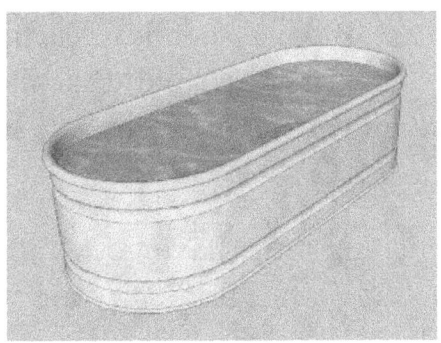

This is also called a quench tub. After an object must have been evacuated from fire, a blacksmith does not start working on it; even if he did not use his bare hands to bring it out, it could still result in injury. It is even more dangerous for a smither to operate on a heated object, perhaps after evacuating with a tong, and he keeps it to cool off.

The reason is that the heated object emits a level of radiation that could last for extended periods; hence it could delay one's work and still cause him some health challenges. It is why you cannot overrule the essential nature of a quench tub.

A quench tub is used to cool off a metal after hours or days of heating. Sometimes different tub is used to cool off a particular metal because of the heat factor in an object.

Quenching or cooling off makes the steel further hardened because of some chemical reactions that occur when cooling. Tubs are eutectoid; this allows for faster hardening and allows metals to cool off starting from a low temperature.

When the quenching must have gotten to its peak, the tub starts bubbling and bringing out vapor, at this process, metals in it become insulated and the heat would reduce very fast. The quench tub or water trough is filled with chemicalized water or oil to contain the heat level that might be present in an object due to excessive firing. Sometimes smithers also use numerous tubs, where the degree of heat supersedes the water temperature.

Workbench

Just as an office worker makes use of an office table to work effectively, store files, accessories and equipment, gadgets, and others, a blacksmith uses the workbench for a similar purpose. A workbench serves the same purpose for his manual work. Whether with a flat surface or a designed surface as it suits the smither, there are provisions in a workbench where tools are also kept.

The workbench is usually wooden made; it can be metalled or adorned with jewelry if the user wishes to, depending on his financial buoyancy. Like an office table, a workbench is rectangular, made up of different components below it.

Aside from knife forging and general forging, a workbench may be used by a smith to cast metal, wield, layout, and grind.

Drill

Its basic function is to make round holes on an object, especially objects that are not easy to penetrate. For an object like a fire-heated metal, in its hardened chemical formation, putting a whole is not easy. This is why you need a highly modernized drill. A metal used for making knives is usually hard and fired; thus, a drill is also an important work tool in a workshop.

Why holes are put in metal are diverse, it helps make the handle of a knife join to a metal so that fasteners and bolt could be driven in easily and many other reasons. Drills may come in a manual form or a mechanical powered form. Because in most cases, a metal used for manufacturing knives is not so strong like metals used for building and the likes. Drills used to produce knives might not be highly sophisticated; an average drill in speed, power, and size would suffice. Some drills are powered through compressed air and electricity.

Due to technological advancement, knife makers can buy cordless drills that could easily be moved and used when recharged. Drills are also important in manufacturing knives because a maker of a knife could improvise on them in other to give his knife a design. Are you looking forward to a neat knife? An automatically powered drill is better than a manual drill due to its accuracy, even though a few of these varieties need some level of financial buoyancy.

Files

In the metal and blacksmithing world, a file is not a compiled book; rather, a file is a tool that reduces a good quantity of materials or substance from an object. Files are hand use and metallic; sometimes, it could come in a square shape, triangle shape, or even round with sharp edges that look like teeth. For easy use, some can be bought with handles attached to them.

It reduces a good amount of materials coercively in an object. In many cases, these materials are often unwanted after a proper design must have been concluded, even to reduce the breadth or length of a metallic object. When a mistake is made during metalwork, files could be used to scrap the mistakes smartly and intelligently.

When making knives, you need to be careful, especially when working on metal, because files are not perfect in clearing mistakes. Notwithstanding, in a circumstance where it happens, a file could help out. Files could also be used to give a metal a curvy like shape, assuming you need a curvy knife, a sharp pointed mouth, and others. Some files have an abrasive surface and a diamond grain tooth.

Belt Grinder

A belt grinder is used to remove unwanted parts of finished metalwork. Furthermore, it is usually used to finish up work in blacksmith workshops or metal factories.

It is belt-like in structure, with an abrasive feature, used on the top of the metal to smoothen it and wipe off unwanted particles on the metal. The belt grinder is broad; it could also trim edges, remove marks gotten during hammering, cleaning, burr removal, metal polishing, washing e.t.c.

Before a blade is packaged or coupled with a handle, a belt grinder runs over it; no wonder knife blades are always smooth, sharp, and neat, cutting through things easily. Some belt grinder includes wide belt grinders, platen belt grinders, stroke belt, back stand, centreless, manual grinders, etc. Belt grinders also help in adjusting the diagonals of a knife blade.

Quenchant

Quenchant is a chemical composition used to quench fire after heating; this is done to obtain a metal component. In instances where a quenchant is used on a knife blade, it further solidifies it and increases its hardness. Quenching is used alongside the water trough; it bubbles in the water trough when a fired metal is dipped inside. It removes heat after coming in direct connection with a metal fired for knife purposes.

Hacksaw

A hacksaw is a version of the normal saw. It has a tooth that is finely designed for cutting metal. Hacksaws are also used for cutting metals. Preference is dependent on the user and his comfortability. It is a very good option to consider for smiths that need to do something lengthy and with a good handle. Hacksaw is not used to smoothen an object but for cutting only. It has a C shaped formed handle; knife manufacturers may comfortably use this in cutting blades for knives.

Angle Grinder

Like the belt grinder, an angle grinder, and also known as a disc grinder, is a handheld power tool for grinding (abrasive cutting) and polishing. It is also used to remove unwanted parts of finished metalwork. It is usually used to finish up work in blacksmith workshops or metal factories. With an abrasive feature, angle grinders are used on the side or angle of metal to smoothen it and likewise wipe off unwanted particles on the metal.

Some of these angle grinders can be manually used, while some are electrical angle grinders. It also helps in adjusting the diagonals of a knife blade. Angle grinders can be used to trim edges, remove marks gotten during hammering, cleaning, burr removal, metal polishing, and washing e.t.c

Knife Making Safety Rules and Equipments

Incidents and unexpected contingencies happen in workshops, especially while mechanized equipment is in use. Fire outbreaks could occur, bruises, heavy cuts, and so on.

Safety precautions and measures are like a first aid that reduces damages when an accident happens suddenly. Some equipment prevents the occurrence of such incidents, which are discussed below alongside the safety measures to follow.

Respirator: During knife making, the air becomes polluted and very dangerous to our kidneys; by mistake, one may breathe in the air mixed with iron particles.

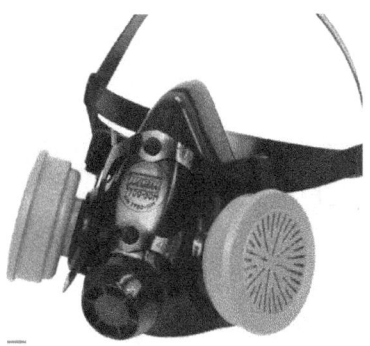

A respirator is important to aid in breathing properly and filtering the air intake. It depends on your choice and financial capability; a respirator may either be disposed of after use or reused after use, but you must adhere strictly to the measures that must be taken before re-suing a respirator.

Safety glasses: Safety glasses are used to prevent flying debris from entering the eye.

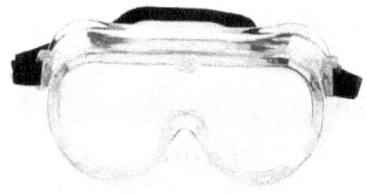

Without this glass, one's eye is predisposed to great danger that may cause blindness or serious visual dysfunction.

Heat resistant apron: During heating and metal firing, the temperature becomes very intense and deadly.

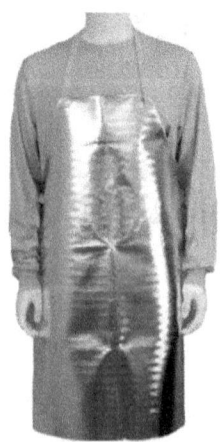

This could result in cancer or skin damage. To prevent such, heat resistant apron should be worn. Most times, it prevents skin burn if by mistake a hot object falls on the body.

Fire extinguisher: The essentiality of a fire extinguisher cannot be overruled.

Fire conflagration could occur during firing, thus the need for an extinguisher.

First aid kits: Where there is any incident that may result in bruises, first aid kits could be helpful to reduce pains.

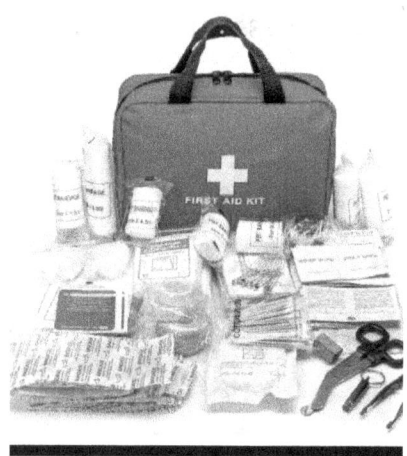

For instance, plaster, pain relief drugs, mentholated spirits, and balms can come very handy in such a situation.

Other safety measures to adhere to are given below:

- Continually checking off equipment if there be any need, servicing machinery, checking of loosed nuts bolts, and providing an alternative exit door.
- Eating foods is not permitted in a workshop, sleeping is highly prohibited, smoking, and frivolous activities. Do not drink during or before working because it is one of the reasons that lead to accidents.

- There should be a provision of enough ventilated space to avoid suffocation, a well-constructed hole, or passage for carbon dioxide-free flow.

As a knife maker, you should go for standard and recommended equipment and tools that support international and best standards and practices. Using substandard saws could cause quick wear, a poor anvil could easily get deformed, and a poorly constructed workbench could break during bladesmithing.

The spacing of equipment is necessary. So while picking an empty room for a workshop, you need to ensure it is spacious enough to some extent. When your tools are too close to each other, it may lead to the breakdown of the tools because the heat transmitted out of one is directly going into another, which reduces the tool's work span. Like a lubricant, well-refined oil is also needed for continuous application on machinery to reduce friction.

Setting Up Your Bladesmithing Workspace

A bladesmith's workplace is his office and should look like one, not a jumble of iron, coal and tools. Everything should be placed in order, and the whole place should be tidy. Starting out for the first time, you need to give your workplace a classic touch as much as possible. The guidelines below will guide you through setting up your bladesmithing workspace.

1. Consider your available space: There is no standard size of a bladesmith workplace; your setup will depend heavily on the amount of space you have available. So before you start drawing plans, consider the space you have available.

2. Choose iron and concrete construction materials: Wood is a bad choice as it can easily be burned by fire. Use concrete and iron as your construction materials.

3. Doors: Determine the size you want to make your door. Make sure your door is wide enough to allow passage of wide and large equipment.

4. Ceiling: Your ceiling's height should be about 8.5-10 feet to allow for easy ventilation and reduce the heat's impact.

5. Ventilation and lighting: Build your workplace in a way that grants you access to natural lighting and ventilation. Make sure your windows are very sizeable and large.

6. A shelf or hanger for your tools: You could create a shelf or wall hanger for your tools or buy an anvil or a workbench that has one.

Chapter 5

Designing Your Knife

Before making a knife, the first step is to sketch or design your knife. You can use graph paper to sketch or design the shape and size of your knife. Endeavor to keep it near the exact size to make the designing process simple.

While you can be creative with your knife design, you should follow the due process to achieve an attractive knife design.

Once you have gotten your preferred knife design, you will need to choose the blade or knife length you want. This decision is solely yours, which means you can choose a long or short knife length. However, take note that a longer knife will need much steel.

Proceed to design the tang (a part of the blade that joins to the handle). Make sure you design a tang you can hold. On the completion of designing your knife's body, you are only moments away from making your knife.

In knife making, designs are extra jobs done after finishing a knife; although it is not compulsory and not found in all knives, they add beauty to one's work. It is borne out of a bladesmith's creative innovation and love of artworks. Some people prefer to employ artists who would help them create designs for different kinds of knives, depending on the purpose.

Designs are not just designs per se, they are very necessary too; they help in giving a bladesmith's knife a unique brand, easy identification of a particular kind of knife, especially when the design is peculiar to knife makers, and it offers help in creating frictions to some extent, necessary while using a knife.

Designs also depend on the knife's purpose. Designs done on a kitchen knife should not be carried out on a combat knife.

Follow the steps below to design a knife:

1. **Sketch the likely knife design on a paper**

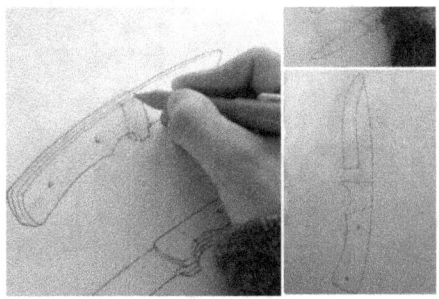

Before making your knife, you need to know the design you want to create. The design of the knife is all dependent on you. Using your pencil, sketch, or draw the design on a piece of paper.

Remember that it is much easier to alter the design on paper rather than on steel.

2. Get your materials ready

The next step requires you to get your materials ready for the knife design process to begin. The design materials can be purchased in a craft store or in any art market.

3. Start designing

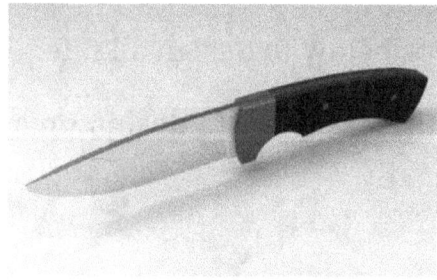

By looking at your earlier sketch, you can easily design your knife to your taste. Endeavor to be careful during the design process on steel because it will be difficult to correct any mistake.

Anatomy of a Knife

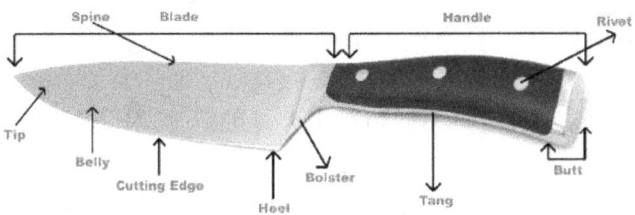

A knife is manufactured from a blade and handle. Usually, it is the cut part of the blade point and shape that govern knife usage. Let's take a brief look at some of the features of a knife, some of which have been discussed in previous chapters.

Spine: The blade spine is the heaviest, unsharpened, and thickest section of a blade. Its job is to support the blade's cutting edge. In addition, it also gives the blade strength to cut things.

Largely, if the spine of a blade is thicker and wider, it will generate more force that can hold inside and downward movement.

Belly: The belly of a blade shows the curved arc that extends towards the outer part along the blade's cutting edge.

Tang: The tang shows the rear or stock blade area that spreads slightly into the handle. Often time, it also covers the handle and it is referred to as full tang.

Serrations: Serrations are the sawtooth style changes include in a few blades. Most times, serrations are positioned in the handle to offer more leverage application.

Bolsters: The bolsters help in the enhancement of the blade's power in the important areas. The important areas include the back of the knife and the handle to blade area. Additionally, the bolster further helps to guard and secure the knife's handle.

Styles of Blade Points

We have gathered several different styles of blade points below. More is discussed in subsequent sections of this chapter. They include:

Spear Point

The spear point is used to denote a blade that has the same geometry on its point. Furthermore, the spear point is also built with two symmetrical edges.

Trailing Point

The trailing point shows a blade where the pointcuts is higher than the surface of the blade spine. In some cases, it may unite or not unite another edge referred to as swage (which holds the designation, whether it is unsharpened or sharpened).

The trailing point is also used in slight and subtle work, including caping game and skinning. Trailing point is a major point for Bowie and hunting styles.

Needle Point

Needle point is also seen as a dagger point. It is the position when a blade contains two symmetrical sharpened blades that join to reach a point.

In contrast to the spear point, which has round edges, a needle point has sharp edges that form a fine point. This makes it perfect for piercing things.

The needle point type blade is usually seen on knives that are used for defending oneself.

Basic Knife Anatomy

Below are some basic knife anatomy to get you started in designing and making your own knife.

Sheepsfoot point: A sheepsfoot point shows a knife that features a well-shaped straight cutting edge.

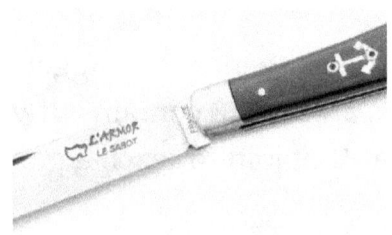

It also features a rounded edge and spine that arrives at the point. A sheepsfoot point knife type is ideal for applications that need increased applied pressure, such as carving wood or cutting textiles.

Clipped point: A clipped point can also mean a slant point. Furthermore, a clipped point is a knife where the rear edge (unsharpened) moves straight along from the handle and ends in the middle.

A clipped point also has a cut-out spot, which can either be curved or straight. Often times, it's called the clip.

Drop point: This is a common blade style. It is mostly seen in several different knife styles. The rear edge (unsharpened) moves straight along from the handle to the upper knife part in a gentle curved way, thereby forming a lowered point.

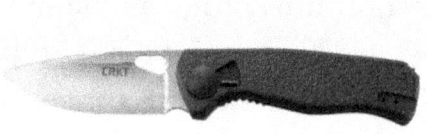

In return, the lowered point offers additional control and gives strength to the knife's tip. Although the tip on a drop point is not as sharp as the tip on a clip point, it is still very strong.

Gut hook: A gut hook is a characteristic of a few hunting knives. It is also seen in numerous different blade portions.

A gut hook's job is to divide the skin of a game in a gutting process while arranging carcasses in a space.

Tanto blade: A tanto blade is gotten from the traditional Japanese swords. It also contains a special 45 degree cut to the upper part. This permits a large amount of force in applying pressure to the spine for stabbing and cutting movements.

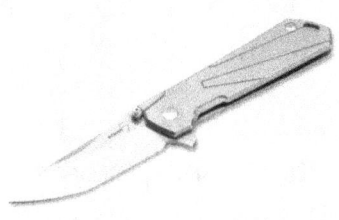

The thick area of the tanto blade features much metal close to the tip. This makes it able to engross the effect from a continuous piercing that would usually break other knives.

Advanced Knife Anatomy

Want a tip on advanced knife making anatomy? Then read below

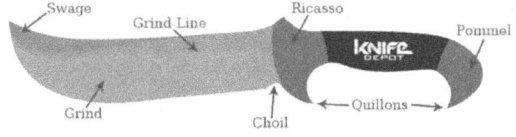

Quillon: The quillon (marked key-own, due to its French origin) is the knife part that creates a horizontal obstacle between the handle and blade, and it is used to

halt one's hand from moving backward or forward on special blades.

Quillon is often seen on large knives and swords. It is also an important factor in swiftly and precisely unsheathing and sheathing the large blades.

Choli: Choli is used to show the blade part where the grind starts and the unsharpened metal stops. It also describes the part between the cutting edge and the tang.

Ricasso: Ricasso is the thick and heavy shank in the front bolster. The front bolster is the knife part that offers support to the blade and also offers a linking point between the handle and blade.

Jimping: Jimping originates from Scottish parlance and North English. This means handsome, slender form, or neat. Jimping is used to show machined cuts or regular patterns on the knife spine. Jimping uses include enhancing grip on the knife's blade for the human thumb when applying downward force.

Cannelure: Often referred to as fuller, it describes a special "I" beam running through the middle of the blade. It lets the knife have a lower weight while holding its general strength. A cannelure is mostly found on larger and longer blades.

Swage: A swage is used to show a functional or decorative edge on the other side of a knife's main edge.

Pommel: The term "**pommel**" is gotten from the French word "**apple**." It describes an ornamental globular mass on the knife's backside. A few knives often include a finger-ring. In simple terms, a finger ring is a characteristic of combat and stylish knives that guard the hand knife by twisting the forefinger to look like a trigger guard.

Blade Profiles of a Knife

This section contains the major blade profiles of a knife which you can factor into when designing your knife. Some of these have been touched on in prior sections of this chapter.

1. **Normal or Simple Blade**

A normal or simple bade feature a straight spine alongside a curving edge that meets to make the knife surface. You can find this on the exact parallel and plane spine.

The long straight knife spine permits you to use the blade with your two hands for safety purposes, especially when using force. Also, it further permits the user to focus their cuts on a small area, which raises the cutting edge's perfection.

The simple blade is perfect for heavy work like cutting heavy roots or batoning wood, and they are great for people looking to develop their knowledge and sharpening skills.

2. **Clip Point Blade**

It features a near similar form to the normal and simple blade because it has a straight spine as well. The only difference between the clip point blade and the normal or simple blade is that close to the blade top is the remaining clipped part; this means there is a part of the blade that looks to be taken away, which forms the blade surface.

The clipped part of the blade can be straight or concave, and it may also have a false edge on the spine, which users can sharpen. The clip point type of blade profile creates a much beautiful needle-like tip to the blade, which makes it perfect for cutting or piercing in tight places.

The tip of the clip point blade is parallel to the spine of the blade or parallel to the middle of the blade. You can find clip point blades from large fix blade hunting to pocket folders. The famous American Bowie is a perfect example of this blade point.

3. Trailing Point Blade

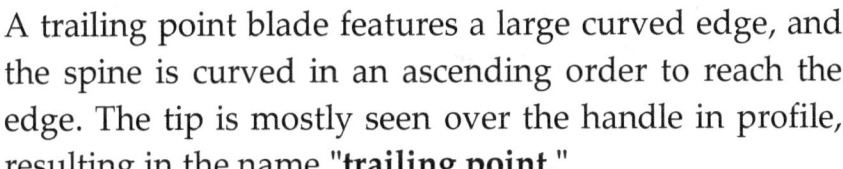

A trailing point blade features a large curved edge, and the spine is curved in an ascending order to reach the edge. The tip is mostly seen over the handle in profile, resulting in the name **"trailing point."**

Additionally, the blade curve permits a higher surface edge, often referred to as a belly, which helps in slashing and slicing long cuts. The trailing point blade is generally used for fillet knives and also slashing weapons.

This blade has a large surface area that joins with the small tip to make it perfect for cutting fish or other little wildlife.

4. Drop Point Blade

A drop point blade features a convex curve to the spine because it goes towards the blade tip. In simple terms, the blade spine begins to drop to the upper part where it reaches the blade curve belly to form the tip.

Going forward, the drop point blade profile forms a blade with a robust and strong tip that is easy to focus on when piercing or cutting.

5. Spear Point Blade

It is seen as a symmetrically pointed blade using an upper part in the same space with the middle line of the blade's alliance. This blade type is mostly made with two edges, and it is mostly used to pierce.

This blade is also referred to as a thrusting weapon.

6. Spey Point Blade

This blade type is a straight-edge blade with an immediate and defined curve near the blade tip. The knife spine is always straight; however, near the blade tip, the spine directs downward to reach the bent edge and creates the blade tip.

This permits the blade tip to be a bit thick and not likely to pierce when carrying out design work. The spey point blade was first made for speying animals, but it is now common in trapper style knives for dressing animals and skinning due to the muted blade tip.

Creating a Knife Template

Templates are important in arriving at a design from a piece of paper on a steel bar. Knife patterns are also ideal for creating knife designs consistently. If you own a template created out of durable materials, you can design numerous knife copies.

You can find numerous pattern types that you could create with many different materials. The first step to take is to design a rough sketch knife design. If you choose to make templates, you don't have to look into anything certain. People can alter the profile of the template whenever it is cut.

Assuming you are designing and manufacturing knives of a similar design, you must get a copy of the initial design. The ideal method is to make knife templates and preserve your artwork.

Follow the steps below on how to make a knife template using different materials.

STEP 1: Paper Pattern

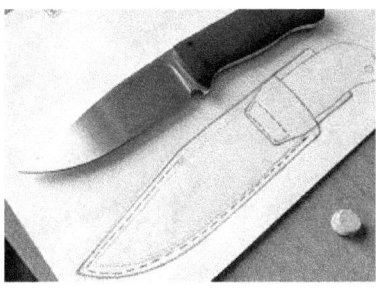

First of all, you have to begin by using a pencil and paper, French curves or a ruler. Then draw the type of design you need on paper. Furthermore, keep on scaling until you arrive at the size you want. Once you've completed that process, it is about time to form a pattern.

If you want to complete this process, stick the paper to plastic or wood and cut and drill the part you need to form a pattern. This process is ideal for creating knives; however, it isn't ideal for creating numerous knives because of its poor durability.

STEP 2: Steel Template

You are allowed to go through the same paper pattern making process using steel. Additionally, you can make paracord knife handle patterns, bowie knife patterns, or case knife patterns if you want. Simply clamp and scribe on the steel and make a long-lasting version.

Use some dyke and paint the upper part of the steel. A marker can also work perfectly to darken the steel. Further, clamp it down and use a carbide scribe and scribe the exterior part of the pattern to form the outline.

Pick it up and place it over the drill and drill it inside the steel. Proceed to drill in a little bit to show where you will drill the main sized holes.

You have the option of using a 30 drill, which is perfect for 8-inch thin material.

You can also transfer or send the knife design template to the blade steel (high stainless carbon or mild steel).

Another option is to use the main cut out and cut the design. People also choose to print out the rough shape cut and use a little spray adhesive to attach it to the steel. You can also use a drip place because the steel will be very hot during the profiling process. While the profiling process is on, use a waterproof on the top.

It's a perfect plan to make patterns, mostly if you'd like to go through the design process once more. Mild steel does not fade because the moisture is a strong one, but if it becomes wet, it will give rise to problems.

Mild steel is sturdy, stable, durable, and cheap, which you can scribe around it several times without damaging the material.

STEP 3: Plexiglass Pattern

If you have already created designs by chance, you can place them and move over to the local store and purchase a piece of Plexiglass. Use a knife and clamp it to the Plexiglas and also use a scribe and sketch a line surrounding it and cut the metal cutting band or woodcutting band soil.

Lastly, drill the same holes in the templates. A Dremel rotary tool can work exceptionally well for this process.

Chapter 6

Forging Method of Knife Making

Understanding and Selecting Steel

When it comes to handmade, asides from doing everything possible to make your knife look perfect, you need to also ensure your knife serves its reason.

In order not to waste time and resources, we have compiled the best ways to understand and select the right steels. Selecting the right knife requires you to focus on the type of steel used to make the blade.

Together with the design and edge geometry, blade steel is also a very important part of a knife because it is critical in how a knife works. Steel is an alloy of iron and carbon added with other elements to enhance some features depending on how you seek to apply it.

Steels come in different types, and it depends on your desired one. Look below to see the crucial characteristics of steel for knife making:

- **Sharpness**

It describes the way the edge of the knife blade cut certain things.

- **Edge holding competency**

The edge retention competency reveals how long the blade will hold its sharpness when people use it for long. Edge retention is mostly talked about, but sadly, the measurement of edge retention does not have a definite set of standards. For most people, edge retention is a joint effort of wear resistance and an edge that holds deformation.

- **Corrosion resistance**

This is the ability to hold corrosion like rust, which is initiated by outer elements such as moisture, salt, and humidity. Be aware that high corrosion resistance requires you to have a general edge performance level.

- **Wear resistance**

This is the ability of the steel to hold the damage from adhesive wear and abrasion. Adhesive wear happens when the debris is displaced from a particular area and joins to another.

On the other hand, abrasive wear happens when the harder particles move on the top of a soft surface. Wear resistance is often linked with the:

- Hardness of steel.
- Ability to hold force/Strength
- Ability to bend without damaging (also referred to as Ductility)
- Workability: This refers to the simplicity at which it can be designed into a different shape

- **Toughness:** This is the ability to absorb or suck in energy without developing cracks.

- **Hardness:** This is the ability to resist deformation whenever the knife is subjected to applied forces. The hardness in knife steels is often linked to strength and it is measured with the Rockwell C scale.

To cater to the numerous needs in knife making, you will always see different steel with any of the below alloys:

- Nickel (includes toughness)
- Chromium (creates corrosion resistant or stainless steel)
- Tungsten (includes wear resistance)
- Cobalt (includes strength)
- Vanadium (includes strength, wear resistance, and hardness)
- Molybdenum (includes corrosion resistance, hardness, and strength)
- Manganese (it makes the steel hard)

Selecting Steel for Knife Making

Selecting the right steel type for making knives is dependent on the result you want. Here are some of the proven ways you can choose steel for your knife making design or project:

Kitchen Knives

If you want to design a kitchen knife, you need to get stainless steel. Stainless steel is also referred to as carbon steel with a touch of chromium to hold corrosion and other things that raise the performance levels, but it has poor or low toughness. Stainless steel is the most common type of steel for EDC knives and it features the likes of 154CM, VG, CTS, 400, MOV, AUS, Crucible SxxV, and Sandvik type of steels. However, the usual stainless steel used to make knives includes 420 cutlery grade stainless steel, 316 surgical grade, common food stainless steel, and 440 higher grade cutlery stainless steel.

NOTE – For stainless steel to be classified as a real one, it must contain a minimum of 13% chromium.

Industrial or Tool Purpose

If you want to design blades used for industrial or tool purposes or if you want to make blades that will balance the advantages and disadvantages of stainless vs. carbon steel, you should make use of tool steel. These are majorly hard steel alloys used for cutting tools. Also, they have high toughness and hardness.

The usual steel tool used to make knives usually contains D2, M2, and A2. In terms of D2, it is not tough; however, it has much higher corrosion resistance and edge retention.

M2 includes a hardness flanking on brittleness; however, it is due to hold or have a beautiful edge.

Other common tool steels in this section are O1, crucible's CPM series, and other highly developed and high-speed steels such as M4.

Machete or Bowie Knife

If you want to make a machete or bowie knife with long durability, you should look into carbon steel. Carbon steels are majorly made and designed for rough surfaces where durability and toughness are necessary. The typical carbon steel used to make knives contains C10_ series steels. The "C" means carbon steel, while the "10" means that they are plain carbon steel having a high 1.00% Manganese in its composition.

Furthermore, the final 2 digits show the percentage of carbon in an alloy. For instance, C1045 will contain 0.45% carbon. It is preferable to opt for medium carbon steels of 0.30% to 0.60% carbon because they have sufficient hardness without turning hard to become so brittle during the knife making process.

Carbon steel's trade-off is likely corrosion because of the low chromium content. However, the most used and wide-spread carbon knife steel is 1095.

Cutting Knife Blanks

After getting the shape you want, the next step is to cut out the knife blanks. For most people, a hacksaw works perfectly to cut out the rough shape in a knife blank, while for others, a bandsaw or any other type of cutting tool will work just fine.

Although the cutting process may take some time, you will be amazed at the outcome when the whole process has been completed. Note that while cutting out the knife blanks, you may end up with a few exciting shaped offcuts

After the cut-out process has been completed, you should clean it up to see the shape.

Grinding the Knife Blanks

With a KMG Knife Grinder, you can grind your knife steel. Simply get a knife grinder and turn it on. Then take your knife blanks or steel and begin placing it on the moving grinder.

In return, the knife grinder will grind your knife to your desired shape. Keep on grinding until you arrive at the shape you want. Grinding knife blanks is one of the easiest methods of shaping a knife, but it is very risky if you are not careful.

Always use a welding glove when grinding the knife steel to avoid injury.

Heat Treating the Knife Blanks

Heat treating is unquestionably the most crucial aspect of making knives. Heat treating is a process in knife making that determines if your knife will resist dropping or when hit on wood.

It is also a challenging process to incorporate as it requires some level of learning and understanding. The best way to attain the best heat is by using a temperature that controls heat treating. You can soak it for 16 minutes, normalize about 3 times and place it into a heat treating oil, and take up to 134.6 degrees F.

Materials and tools to heat treat knife blanks

- **Air source**

You can use a semi-broken blow dryer or heat gun, depending on the available one.

- **Magnet**

This is used for testing or checking the temperature of the steel. It works by touching the magnet to the steel, but you need to be extra careful so as not to burn yourself.

- **Charcoal**

Most people often use natural hardwood lump charcoal for this process. Basically, any charcoal that can get hot instantly and for a long time is advisable to be used.

- **Quenching oil**

You have some options of oil available to be used. Depending on your budget, you can choose to get cheap or expensive oil. The likes of peanut oil, olive oil, motor oil, and vegetable oil can work exceptionally well.

- **Heat resistant container**

This tool is used to retain the oil for quenching. This method of heat treating a knife blank will work perfectly with simple and easy high carbon steels of 1095, 1085, 1080, 1090, 5160, and the likes.

Forge

After getting your materials in place, the next step is forging. You don't need to go deep into the forging process because you only need some bricks prepared in a circle format while having an opening on a side for air to enter. However, if you are financially buoyant, you could use a gas forge.

Begin your forge

The subsequent step is to begin your forge properly. You can load up your brick box with lump charcoal, get your hairdryer in position and fire it up.

Afterward, leave it for some minutes to heat up. Once it gets to about 2500 degrees Fahrenheit, melt steel in a crude forge, but you will need a welding glove for this process.

While being patient for the forge to meet up with the required temperature, it's important to ready your quench. Pick up your oil in your heat resistant container and pre-heat it to reach 130 degrees Fahrenheit.

Heat the knife blanks

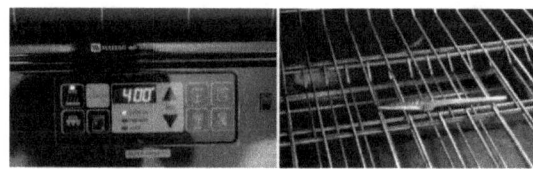

Once you are done heating your forge, proceed and stick the knife inside. Here is where the challenging part arises; you would have to regulate the temperature with a charcoal forge or a gas forger, especially if you want to create a large blade.

You also need to watch and be cautious when heating the steel. Do not try to overheat the knife blanks, or else it may not come out well. While heating it, look to see the steel color.

You can test the temperature by placing salt on the blade. The reason is that salt melts at 1474 degrees, so once it melts, you will know if it has reached the main temperature.

Quench

Once you are fine with the blade and its high temperature, you will have to remove it quickly. Since you won't want to lose enough heat, you are advised to immediately take out the knife and plunge it into the oil.

Most people prefer to put and remove the knife into the oil to break up any air bubbles that may be inside it. To be sure if the steel is already hardened, simply pick up a file and scrape the edge of the file across the knife. If, by chance, the knife is already hardened, you will find it firm than the file.

Tempering

After the quenching process has been completed, the steel will be so hard. Since the steel is so hard to turn into a knife, you will have to heat the blanks once more to reach about 400 degrees. This process removes the stress in the steel and makes it soft a little.

There are different tempering methods, but the most used method is to place it in the oven to reach about 400 degrees for two cycles at 60 minutes, which will let the knife become cool in between the two cycles.

Roundup

It's time to round up your knife heating blank process. You can easily do this by sanding the entire body and closing up the grind.

Alternatively, you can include handle scales and any other attractive thing to your knife to design and make it beautiful.

Making a Handle for the Knife

A knife handle is important for holding or getting a grip on a knife. You can easily make your custom knife handle if you have the materials and tools in place.

Here are the important materials needed to make a knife handle

- Masking tape
- Scales
- Knife blade
- Epoxy
- Sandpaper

The machines used during the process of making knife handles include:

- Clamps
- Wood band saw
- Files
- Drill press
- Metal sanders

- Metal band saw
- Woodshop sanders
- Scribe

Elective materials to get include:

- Color spacers
- Pins

Follow the steps below to make a knife handle:

1. Prepare your materials

Place your materials on a clean surface, unsheathe your blade and close the sharp part of the blade in masking tape. The essence of this is to protect your hands from being cut and the blade from getting damaged.

The next step is to gather your handle scales and cut them to a square having 5.1 inches of additional material close to the blade handle. You can use a pencil to sketch the edge of the blade handle on your handle scales.

You can use the vertical band saw to cut out your desired shape handle.

2. Drill the pinholes

Knife handles usually have predrilled holes. These holes reveal where you can input your pins as well as the pin size. If you cannot attain the right pin size, you can use a drill.

You need to tape your two scales and join them together before taping your blade handle on the top. Spot the scale spots where the pin will be headed to. If this process is not done the right way, you might experience problems gathering your knife.

The subsequent process is to select the drill but a bit larger than the usual pin. Further, clamp down your scale and drill a long vertical pinhole. You can drill a hole at both ends and drill a hole close to the blade and in the middle hole. Go through the same steps for the second scale.

In a case whereby your knife has rivets and not pins, you must countersink your hole to get your preferred depth. A caliper works fine to know the rivet head size.

Do not epoxy your blade together without shaping and sanding the part of the scale that will reach the sharp edge of the blade. Also, ensure you do not forget to line up the two scales symmetrically if you need your handle front to match both sides.

If you decide to include a color spacer in the blade, you need to drill the holes in the piece.

3. **Cut your desired pin size**

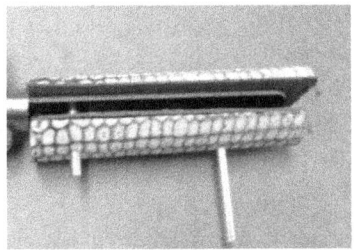

To cut your pin size, simply place your handle together and allow the end of the pin to show out of the handle a 1/8th. Sketch 1/8th on the longest part and cut out your preferred pin on the metal band saw to the correct length. It is much more advisable to cut your pins longer and not closer.

4. Epoxy the blade handle together

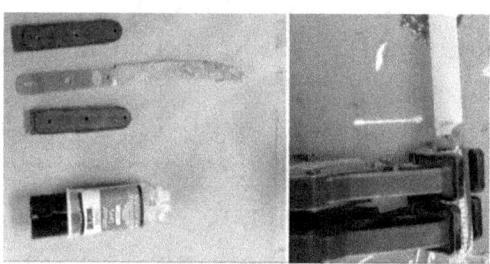

While in the paint booth, take two clamps and put out a new piece of paper on a surface. Ensure the pins move into the holes you have already drilled.

The next step requires you to prepare or assemble your epoxy and use a brush to apply a constant coat and light of the epoxy on the top of your scale handle. Join it to the metal blade handle. Furthermore, push the pins into the drilled holes and place the metal and wood in their right position.

Lastly, epoxy the other side of the handle scale and attach it on the top of the outer pins to the other side of the metal handle. On the completion of epoxying the entire layers, use two clamps to fasten the knife handle together.

Be sure you wait for a minimum of 5 minutes but ensure you remove it before it dries.

5. Sand your blade handle into shape

This is the step that gets you closer to creating the shape of your knife handle. Now, get the flow or design of how you want your knife to look like. Your knife handle shape depends on your taste, as you could have one with a thin handle or wide handle.

Once you have gotten the shape you desire, you can proceed to polish your knife handle.

6. Polish your knife handle

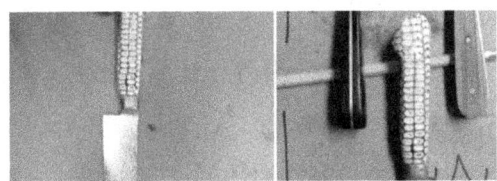

Any recommended wood polish can polish your knife handles. For some people, 600 and 400 grit sandpaper works to polish the surface of the handgrip.

Use the wood polish on your wood and sand down. Once done, go through the process again and allow it to stay until the next day.

7. Finishing

After you handle has dried successfully, you can include any type of finishes you prefer and take out the tape around the sharp end of your knife blade. Once done, you have prepared your knife handle and begin using it the way you want.

Sharpening and Caring for Your Knife

Cutting things with a dull knife can be a time waster and dangerous. Luckily, there is no complexity in sharpening and taking care of your knife.

Follow the steps below to sharpen your knife using a diamond stone or whetstone:

1. Select an angle to sharpen your knife

If you are aware of the angle your knife is sharpened at, you may want to sharpen the same angle once more. Sharpening at dissimilar angles will require added time, and some portions may be rough before you arrive at a smooth surface.

- In case you are not aware of the present sharpening angle of your knife, you can ask your knife manufacturer to ask a knife shop owner.
- Meanwhile, if you choose to make a drastic choice, you can select an angle of 10 degrees to 30 degrees per slide. Shallow angles produce a sharp edge that is not durable, while steeper angles are long-lasting.

2. Lubricate your diamond stone or whetstone using a little amount of mineral oil

You can get honing oil, which is a light type of mineral oil that will lubricate your stone while making it easy for the knife blade to move over the stone.

3. Use an angle guide to manage your edge's angle

If you are with a sharpening guide, it may aid you in controlling your edge's angle. It is a minor instrument that is positioned beneath the knife to get a straight or right angle when scraping the knife across the face of the stone.

One out of many challenging processes of sharpening a knife is arriving at the correct angle. In order to make this process straightforward and simple, try to paint the tip of both blade sides using a sharpie pen.

4. Begin on the rough grit portion of the stone

Look at the grit on your stone to know the correct part. Most diamond stones and whetstones feature dissimilar grits on the two sides. The fine grit part is used to hone or sharpen the knife, while the rough side is used to grind the steel down.

The grinding part should supersede others, and that is why you need to begin on the rough grit side.

5. To gain an asymmetrical edge, simply sharpen the knife by dragging it across the stone on the other side where you need to cut a thin part from the stone

This process gives room for burr to make and offer durability status.

6. **Keep on grinding with the same angle until your grind is rough through the steel**

There is no need to make this step perfect; simply make a very good estimation exercise.

7. **Flip the knife over and hone the opposite blade side until you form a new edge**

The best way to know that you have taken out sufficient metal is to hone until you have gotten a burr. A burr is often too little to see; however, you can touch it by scraping it on your thumb.

8. **Flip the stone over and start sharpening a part of the blade**

In this step, you will be focusing on the better grit. You aim to smooth and remove the burrs formed by sharpening the knife over the coarser grit. This will change the blade edge from a ground edge into a honed and finer edge.

9. **Start changing swipes on the fine grit**

It is important to hone a part of the knife with one stroke and quickly flip the knife and hone the other part. Carry out this process on multiple occasions to gain the best outcome.

You may choose to polish the edge to gain your best sharpness.

Another method of sharpening a knife is by using a sharpening bar or sharpening steel. Follow the steps below to use a honing rod to sharpen your knife:

1. **Use the rod in the middle of your sharpening from reducing your blade's quality**

The sharpening rod or sharpening steel is basically used to raise and sharpen a blunt blade. Its job is to realign the steel in a blade while touching a little part and removing the flat parts.

2. **Use the honing rod in your less dominant hand**

You are required to hold the honing rod in a comfortable manner and an angle away from your skin. Furthermore, the rod up should be raised higher than the rod grip.

3. **Hold the knife tightly on your main hand**

You should grip the knife tightly and place your thumb on the back of the knife, away from the blade part.

4. Hold your knife at roughly 20 degrees

You don't need the angle to be similar; you can always estimate it. Depending on the angle you select, ensure you maintain the exact angle all through the sharpening process.

If you alter the angle you previously used, the metal in the blade will not come out smooth.

5. Maintain a 20-degree angle, and take the knife across the higher half of the honing rod

Begin this movement with the heel of the knife coming in contact with the rod and close it with the tip of the knife touching the rod.

To become a professional here, you have to move your hand, arm, and wrist. If you don't move your wrist, it would be difficult to sweep the whole blade.

6. Maintain a 20-degree angle, and take the knife across the lower half of the honing rod

With a similar sweep of your wrist, hands, and arm, slowly take the knife across the lower half of the rod. You can use little force as regards to the weight.

How to care for your knife and keep them sharpened

Often, we complain that our knives have lost their sharpness, but we fail to realize we must care for our knives and keep them sharpened every time.

The below list contains the ways to keep your knife safe and sharpened:

- Do not take them up (knives) to hit saw or turkey joints through frozen things.
- Endeavor to always use a plastic or wooden cutting board. Do not try to chop your vegetables on steel, glass, granite, ceramic, or a hard surface.
- Wash differently in hot water, and never leave your knife in too much water.
- Also, try not to soak them in a sink or keep them in a puddle of tomato puree. Although knives are made from stainless steel, they are easily susceptible to corrosion.

- Don't keep them in a drawer. Instead, use edge protectors or a knife block.
- Try to hone or heat your knives regularly.
- Re-sharpen them annually (two times or more).
- Try not to over sharpen your knife, else you might be destroying its steels
- Don't hone your knife using a can-opener sharpener.
- Keep your knives clean and dry.
- Finish using a wonderful gritstone. This will improve your knife and make them way sharper than you think.

Chapter 7

Troubleshooting Common Knife Making Problems

While trying to forge and make a knife during your leisure time or for business purposes, you may run into some problems. It is important not to panic whenever you encounter issues when making knives because a majority of the outlined issues can be corrected easily.

We have compiled the common knife making challenges and resolutions. After reading this section, you should have a smooth ride while making more knives.

1. Knife failed to harden

If your knife failed to become hard after heating it, there is a cause for worry. However, there are numerous reasons why your knife may fail to harden. These reasons include the following:

- Not sufficient carbon in the steel.
- Incorrect austenitizing temperature: You can solve this issue by using a temperature controller.

Simply set the temperature to 25 degrees or use table salt or magnet to move nearer.
- A layer of decarburized steel on the exterior part of your knife because of forging. Solve this problem by grinding a bit more and try it once more.
- Incorrect quench for the steel: You don't expect all liquid to harden with every steel. Endeavor to always use a quicker quench liquid to get the correct steel quench.

2. Tempering very hot

The outcome of this problem is that the knife will appear soft as well. When this occurs, ensure you use the two-cycle process by producing the first 25-50 degrees and the second one a bit lower.

3. Spaces between handle and tang

This problem is the outcome of the surface not being smooth. It is either the scales or the tang are not flat or smooth. Get this solved by using a flat disk or surface plate to smoothen them.

4. Handles appearing to loose

This is usually due to the low surface arrangement. Oil on the tang; and this includes fingerprints; hence, the glue fails to stick. Individuals can correct this problem by using denatured alcohol or acetone to clean the tang and erase it with clean water.

While doing this, ensure the scales and tangs are flat and clean. Also, ensure you use effective glue during the whole process.

5. Rough plunge cuts

A rough plunge cut is a result of a starter's work. If you experience an uneven or rough plunge cut, using a file guide can correct the issue. Simply ensure you scribe the middle line before you seek to grind.

Further, try grinding your last plunge cuts after heat treating your knife. Creating even plunge cuts is a problematic and thought-provoking knife making processes. Although you may make mistakes during your beginning stage, you can master the art after a short time.

6. Scratches showing after polish

After polishing your knife, are you still seeing scratches? Well, its causes are usually attributed to poor underlying grind.

The only solution to solving issues of visible scratches after polishing is returning to a minimum of 120 grits and polishing your knife once more. Now, ensure you get all the former grit scratches before you proceed to the subsequent grit.

If you will polish using the hand sanding process, ensure you are changing directions with each grit modification and attempting to get a flash of good lightning.

7. Handle material burns

Are your handle materials burning or changing colors while shaping? This simply shows you are plying the wrong route by using light materials such as maple.

The main cause of burning handle materials or changing colors is that the belt runs fast. This problem can be corrected by changing to a coarser belt, slower speed, or a fresh belt.

8. A dark ring showing in the handle pins

It is due to round holes or oversized roles whereby the glue enters the gap and displays a ring.

Alternatively, this problem could also result from grinding your pin stock down way quicker to burn a dark ring in your handle material.

9. Divot in the blade flats

This issue arises as a result of tipping the blade to the area. Solve this issue by moving back to 120 grit and grind it out while the blade stays away from any divots.

10. Edge chipping

Edge chipping shows that your edge is too brittle and caused by low normalization before the quench is too hard. Assuming the edge is chippy, you can attempt tempering 25 degrees much higher. It might be effective, especially if the brittleness has low-temperature control when heating up.

11. Edge rolling

Edge rolling clearly shows that your edge is too soft. It occurs when the tempering is too hot or not being able to become hard. You cannot find a straightforward process of fixing edge rolling issues. The only proven solution is to heat the treatment once more.

12. Problem with warpage

Sometimes, the blade might emerge from the quench crooked. On second thought, it's always straightened hot, higher than 500 degrees, once the quench is done. You should pick up a welding glove and use it.

Leave it to turn cool, and once it is cool, you can straighten it while carrying out the tempering cycle. Simply clamp the blade to the flat or smooth steel. Follow the temper cycles like you normally would do. This process may need you to fail before you become perfect; however, it is an ideal method to become successful. Assuming you are seeking a two-piece knife, proceed and straighten one side cold.

The end... almost!

Hey! We've made it to the final chapter of this book, and I hope you've enjoyed it so far.

If you have not done so yet, I would be incredibly thankful if you could take just a minute to leave a quick review on Amazon

Reviews are not easy to come by, and as an independent author with a little marketing budget, I rely on you, my readers, to leave a short review on Amazon.

Even if it is just a sentence or two!

Customer Reviews

☆☆☆☆☆ 2
5.0 out of 5 stars ▾

5 star	▀▀▀▀▀▀	100%
4 star		0%
3 star		0%
2 star		0%
1 star		0%

Share your thoughts with other customers

[Write a customer review]   ⬅

See all verified purchase reviews ›

So if you really enjoyed this book, please...

>> Click here to leave a brief review on Amazon.

I truly appreciate your effort to leave your review, as it truly makes a huge difference.

Chapter 8

Knife Making Frequently Asked Questions (Q&A)

There are frequently asked questions by readers and beginners who just started knife making or intend to start knife making. This chapter is geared toward answering some of these frequently asked questions borne out of personal experience as well as those of experts.

Q - How does one know how good a steel is?

Answer: Purchasing of steel could vary in its durability in a few cases; however, how good a steel is will depend on how heated and treated it is during the process of making knives.

Q - Time limit of firing and heating?

Answer: Well, this depends on individual choices and preference. You must also know that if a metal is heated well, it will turn fine. Regardless, a moderate amount of heating would suffice.

Q - Where can I purchase an already designed iron?

Answer: Some metals already have been designed or probably heated; you would get them in a craft store. On the other hand, assuming you decide to heat the metal again before making the knife, getting a plain metal without design would be better.

After all, during hammering, you could put your design and thereafter fire up.

Q - Which serves best when it comes to buying knife making equipment, manual or automatic?

Answer: It all depends on financial abilities; automatic/electrical equipment is not too stressful. However, manuals are stressful and less financially demanding. Electrically powered equipment is too tasking financially.

Q - Are there any health challenges concerning making knives?

Answer: You can find several health implications while making knives. For example, dust is emitted during the process, which may not be so good for an asthmatic patient, some bruises and injuries, and coughs are gotten during the making process.

Q - How can I solve health challenges that may arise from making knives?

Answer: People who might be susceptible to a few health implications, such as those above, need to stop making knives immediately. Asthmatic patients should not bother risking it. For things like cough and catarrh, a nose mask could ameliorate the effect. Injuries, bruises could be prevented through proper caution and ensuring the various equipment are well kept and well serviced to prevent life-threatening occurrences.

Q - What other solutions could one follow there is an interest in making knives?

Answer: Where a person is financially buoyant, he may set up the business, provide the equipment, and also employ those who would engage in the process of making knives.

Q – How can I learn the process of making knives?

Answer: Well, you are already reading a guide on knife making. You can further your knowledge in this craft from different ebook guides on knife making, physical books, and enrolling in online courses.

Q - Besides reading books, what other things are needed to further increase my knife making understanding?

Answer: There are opportunities to go for internship training in a notable knife making factory, engage in masterclasses, etc.

Q - What is the financial estimate to open a workshop?

Answer: Opening a workshop could be relative to an individual financially. Thus, it is imperative to put into consideration your financial prowess.

The workshop standards also play an important role when considering opening a workshop especially where automatically powered machine and electrical work tools would be used, which would require a high amount of cash.

With this explanation, you cannot find a specific financial estimate.

Q - Where can I obtain knife making tools for purchase?

Answer: Knife making tools can be gotten in different local markets around you; some markets deal on equipment specifically. In fact, intending buyers prefer to discuss with sellers about their preference.

You can further make some orders online because many companies and stores now have internet outlets where knife tool displays are done.

Q - What are the things to look out for when purchasing equipment?

Answer: The question to this answer is reliant on the intending buyer; you could take out time on researches and conclude the versions and models of your choice.

Q – What is the amount of space needed for a workshop?

Answer: A relatively large space is enough, with good ventilation and adequate room temperature too.

Q - What is the financial benefit of producing knives yourself?

Answer: You produce it at a manufacturing cost price, unlike buying knives from a retail store, where the costs might have been padded already. You could also sell to others, thus making extra gains.

Q - Can I actually make a personal creative design?

Answer: Yes, knife makers can add designs and carvings during the manufacturing process.

Conclusion

Although knife making is a complex art and undoubtedly the leading profit-making skill one can acquire, beginners can still be equipped by reading books such as this on how to start making knives either for personal or business purposes.

As explained, Knife making requires using some machinery for production, contingent on the method the knife maker wishes to use.

It is an elitist art that many people have not yet explored; thus, there is an increasing demand for knife makers and knives in general in the market. Individuals can find several knives for production; for example, there are kitchen knives, knives for eating, and others.

For the beginners who have faced confusion regarding going about knife making, this book is a comprehensive learning course that will help you get started in making your own knife through forging as well as educate you on other important tips and guidelines needed, such as purchasing your tools, safety rules to adhere to, and starting your knife making business the right way, among others.

I wish you the very best in your knife making journey.

Happy bladesmithing, bladesmiths!